PIVOT & PUSH

Through Life-Changing Moments

PIVOT & PUSH

Through Life-Changing Moments

DR. SHAMEL Y. ROLLE-SANDS

UNIVERSAL IMPACT PRESS

Published by Universal Impact Press. www.UniversalImpactPress.com

This journal is intended for spiritual reflection and personal growth. It is not a substitute for professional medical, psychological, legal, or financial advice. If you are experiencing a crisis or require professional support, please consult a qualified professional.

ISBN: 978-1-956711-93-6

CONTENTS

Introduction 1
Embracing Transformation Through Faith

How to use this journal 5

Week 1 9
Finding Your Pivot Point

1. Day 1 10
   A New Beginning
2. Day 2 12
   The Power of Perspective
3. Day 3 14
   Seeking Divine Guidance
4. Day 4 16
   Self-Awareness
5. Day 5 18
   Humility
6. Day 6 20
   Surrender
7. Day 7 22
   Sabbath Rest

Week 1 Recap 24

Week 2 27
Pushing Past Obstacles

8. Day 8 28
Overcoming Obstacles

9. Day 9 30
Enduring Hardship

10. Day 10 32
Resilience

11. Day 11 34
Perseverance

12. Day 12 36
Faith

13. Day 13 38
Hope

14. Day 14 40
Strength in Christ

Week 2 Recap 42

Week 3 45
Cultivating Inner Peace

15. Day 15 46
Finding Peace in the Storm

16. Day 16 48
Practicing Gratitude

17. Day 17 50
Mindfulness

18. Day 18 52
Forgiveness

19. Day 19 54
Self-Care

20. Day 20 56
Meditation

21. Day 21 58
Be Still

Week 3 Recap 60

Week 4 63
Embracing God's Purpose

22. Day 22 64
Discovering Your God-Given Purpose

23. Day 23 66
Stepping Out in Faith

Fullpage image 67

24. Day 24 68
Surrendering Control

25. Day 25 70
Purpose in Challenges

26. Day 26 72
Serving Others

27. Day 27 74
Living Intentionally

28. Day 28 76
Embracing Your Identity in Christ

Week 4 Recap 78

Closing Message 79
Your Journey Continues

About the Author 82

INTRODUCTION

EMBRACING TRANSFORMATION THROUGH FAITH

Your 28-Day Journey of Spiritual Renewal

Welcome, brave traveller, to a transformative 28-day expedition of spiritual, personal, and professional growth. This is not just a journal—it's a compass for your soul, a roadmap through life's most challenging terrains, designed to help you navigate with grace, resilience, and unwavering faith.

The Power of Perspective and Perseverance

At the heart of this journey lies the **PIvOT** and **PUSH** framework—a powerful approach to personal transformation that will become your spiritual and practical guide:

PIvOT: The art of shifting perspectives, transforming adversity into opportunity

PUSH: The courage to persist, to press forward despite obstacles, to move beyond your current limitations

What Awaits You

A Holistic Approach to Growth

This journal is meticulously crafted to engage you on multiple levels:

Spiritual Depth: Drawing wisdom from Proverbs, Psalms, and other scriptural sources

Emotional Resilience: Developing tools to process and overcome challenges

Practical Transformation: Implementing actionable strategies for personal and professional growth

Your Daily Companions

Each day, you will discover:

Carefully selected scripture passages

Powerful, introspective prayers

Thought-provoking reflections

Practical journaling exercises

The Journey's Architecture

The journal is strategically structured into four transformative weeks:

Week 1: Finding Your Pivot Point

Week 2: Pushing Past Obstacles

Week 3: Cultivating Inner Peace

Week 4: Embracing God's Purpose

Your Commitment, God's Transformation

This journey requires your active participation. By consistently engaging with these pages, you will:

Develop a deeper, more intimate relationship with God

Cultivate a resilient, positive mindset

Learn to see challenges as opportunities for growth

Transform your spiritual, personal, and professional landscape

A Personal Invitation

This is more than a journal—it's an invitation to radical transformation. An opportunity to rewrite your story, to **PIvOT** from limitation to possibility, and to **PUSH** through whatever holds you back.

Are You Ready?

Take a deep breath. Open your heart. Turn the page.

Let's begin this transformative journey together.

With faith, hope, and anticipation,

Let's begin this transformative journey together!

HOW TO USE THIS JOURNAL

YOU'VE TAKEN THE DEEP breath. You've opened your heart. Now let's talk about how to walk this journey, one day at a time.

Over the next 28 days, you will be guided through a rhythm of scripture, reflection, prayer, and journaling—each one building on the last, each one drawing you closer to the transformation God has already prepared for you.

Your Daily Rhythm

Set aside 15–20 minutes in a quiet place where you can be fully present. Each day follows the same pattern:

Scripture — Read the day's passage slowly. Let it settle before you move on.

Reflection — Sit with the question. There are no wrong answers here—only honest ones.

Prayer — Use the written prayer as a starting point, then continue the conversation with God in your own words.

Journaling Prompt — Write freely. Don't worry about perfection. This space is between you and God.

The Four Weeks Ahead

As you read in the Introduction, this journal moves through four intentional stages of growth:

Week 1: Finding Your Pivot Point — Slow down, seek God's direction, and develop the self-awareness to recognize where change must begin.

Week 2: Pushing Past Obstacles — Build the resilience, perseverance, and faith you need to press through whatever stands in your way.

Week 3: Cultivating Inner Peace — Practice gratitude, forgiveness, and stillness as you learn to trust God's timing for your life.

Week 4: Embracing God's Purpose — Step boldly into your calling, living with intention and anchored in your identity in Christ.

A Word of Grace

Consistency matters more than perfection. If you miss a day, give yourself grace and pick up where you left off. This is not a test—it is a conversation with God about where you've been and where He is leading you.

Now, turn the page. Day 1 is waiting for you.

WEEK 1

Reflection

WEEK 1

FINDING YOUR PIVOT POINT

WELCOME TO WEEK 1! This week focuses on self-discovery, spiritual alignment, and understanding personal growth. The key themes include:

- Trusting in God's guidance and timing
- Shifting perspectives to find joy and peace
- Developing self-awareness and understanding personal strengths and weaknesses
- Cultivating humility and surrendering control to God
- Learning to rest and recharge spiritually

The daily reflections encourage journaling about life changes, perspective shifts, seeking divine guidance, and understanding oneself. You are invited to explore their inner landscape, acknowledging both challenges and opportunities for growth through prayer, scripture, and introspective writing.

DAY 1

A New Beginning

SCRIPTURE: PROVERBS 3:5-6 ENCOURAGES complete trust in God to realign priorities and guide every step:

"Trust in the Lord completely, and do not rely on your own opinions. With all your heart rely on Him to guide you, and He will lead you in every decision you make."

Reflection: What areas of your life feel out of balance? How can you trust in God's guidance to realign your priorities?

Prayer: *Father, help me to trust in Your perfect timing and Your sovereign plan. Give me the wisdom to discern Your will and the courage to make necessary changes.*

Journaling Prompt: Write about a time when you experienced a significant life change. How did you respond? What did you learn from the experience?

DAY 2

The Power of Perspective

Scripture: Proverbs 15:15 highlights the power of perspective and choosing joy amid challenges:

Everything seems to go wrong when you feel weak and depressed, but when you choose to be cheerful, every day will bring you more and more joy and fullness.

Reflection: How can you shift your perspective to find joy and peace in any situation?

Prayer: *Father, help me to see things from Your perspective. Give me a heart of gratitude and a spirit of contentment.*

Journaling Prompt: Write about a recent challenge you faced. How did your perspective on the situation change over time?

DAY 3

SEEKING DIVINE GUIDANCE

SCRIPTURE: PSALM 37:5 URGES surrender to God's guidance for peace and clarity:

Give God the right to direct your life, and as you trust Him along the way, you'll find He pulled it off perfectly!

Reflection: How can you seek God's guidance in every decision you make?

Prayer: *Father, guide my steps and direct my path. Help me to listen to Your voice and follow Your lead.*

Journaling Prompt: Write about a time when you felt lost or confused. How did God guide you through that experience?

DAY 4

Self-Awareness

SCRIPTURE: Proverbs 14:10 promotes self-awareness and understanding one's own unique emotional journey:

The heart knows its own bitterness, and no one else can share its joy.

Reflection: How well do you know yourself? What are your strengths and weaknesses?

Prayer: *Father, help me to see myself as You see me. Give me the humility to acknowledge my flaws and the courage to embrace my strengths.*

Journaling Prompt: Write about your personality traits, both positive and negative. How can you use your strengths to overcome your weaknesses?

DAY 5

Humility

Scripture: Proverbs 22:4 focuses on the rewards of humility and submission to God:

Laying your life down in tender surrender before the Lord will bring life, prosperity, and honor as your reward.

Reflection: How can you cultivate humility in your daily life?

Prayer: *Father, help me to be humble and teachable. Give me the grace to serve others and to submit to Your authority.*

Journaling Prompt: Write about a time when you had to humble yourself. What did you learn from the experience?

DAY 6

SURRENDER

SCRIPTURE: MATTHEW 6:33 ENCOURAGES seeking God's kingdom first for provision and purpose:

"So above all, constantly chase after the realm of God's kingdom and the righteousness that proceeds from Him. Then all these less important things will be given to you abundantly."

Reflection: How can you surrender your worries and anxieties to God?

Prayer: *Father, I surrender my life to You. Help me to trust in Your plan and to let go of control.*

Journaling Prompt: Write about a situation in which you felt overwhelmed or stressed. How did you surrender your worries to God?

DAY 7

SABBATH REST

SCRIPTURE: EXODUS 20:8-11 REMINDS of the importance of rest and devotion to God:

"Remember the Sabbath day by keeping it holy. Six days you shall labor and do all your work, but the seventh day is a sabbath to the Lord your God."

Reflection: How can you rest and recharge in God's presence?

Prayer: *Father, help me to rest and rejuvenate in Your presence. Give me peace and tranquillity.*

Journaling Prompt: Write about your ideal Sabbath day. How can you incorporate rest and relaxation into your weekly routine?

WEEK 1 RECAP

THIS WEEK FOCUSED ON self-discovery, spiritual alignment, and learning to trust God's guidance. You were invited to slow down, reflect inwardly, and recognize areas of your life that may need realignment.

This week encouraged you to:

- Trust God's direction rather than relying solely on your own understanding
- Shift your perspective to find peace and clarity
- Develop greater self-awareness and humility
- Practice surrender and embrace intentional rest

Closing Reflection:
As you move forward, remember that meaningful change begins with awareness and a willingness to trust God's leading, even when the path ahead is unclear.

WEEK 2

Realignment

WEEK 2

Pushing Past Obstacles

Welcome to Week 2! This week is dedicated to building resilience, perseverance, and faith in the face of challenges. Focus areas include:

- Overcoming obstacles with God's help
- Finding hope and comfort during difficult times
- Developing resilience and the ability to bounce back from setbacks
- Maintaining focus on long-term goals
- Strengthening faith and finding hope amid despair
- Relying on Christ's strength to overcome personal challenges

The journaling prompts and prayers are designed to help you reflect on past challenges, learn from them, and develop strategies to persist through current and future obstacles. The emphasis is on spiritual and personal empowerment.

DAY 8

Overcoming Obstacles

SCRIPTURE: PROVERBS 24:16 ENCOURAGES resilience and faith in God's strength to overcome repeated obstacles:

For the lovers of God may suffer adversity and stumble seven times, but they will continue to rise over and over again. But the unrighteous are brought down by just one calamity and will never rise again.

Reflection: What obstacles are currently hindering your progress? How can you overcome them with God's help?

Prayer: *Father, give me the strength to persevere through difficult times. Help me to trust in Your promises and to keep pressing forward.*

Journaling Prompt: Write about a time when you faced a significant obstacle. How did you overcome it? What lessons did you learn?

DAY 9

Enduring Hardship

Scripture: Psalm 34:17-18 offers comfort in God's nearness during hardship:

The Lord hears His people when they call to Him for help. He rescues them from all their troubles. The Lord is close to the brokenhearted; He rescues those whose spirits are crushed.

Reflection: How can you find hope and comfort during suffering?

Prayer: *Father, be my refuge and strength. Help me to find peace in Your presence.*

Journaling Prompt: Write about a time when you felt discouraged or defeated. How did you find strength to keep going?

DAY 10

Resilience

Scripture: Psalm 27:1 encourages boldness and hope in God's protection:

The Lord is my revelation-light to guide me along the way; He's the source of my salvation to defend me every day. I fear no one!

Reflection: How can you develop resilience in the face of adversity?

Prayer: *Father, give me the strength to endure hardship and the courage to bounce back from setbacks.*

Journaling Prompt: Write about a time when you showed resilience in the face of a challenge. What helped you persevere?

DAY 11

PERSEVERANCE

SCRIPTURE: PROVERBS 13:4 EMPHASIZES diligence and persistence in pursuing goals:

The slacker wants it all and ends up with nothing, but the hard worker ends up with all that he longed for.

Reflection: How can you stay focused on your goals, even when it gets tough?

Prayer: *Father, help me to be persistent and determined. Give me the motivation to keep pressing forward.*

Journaling Prompt: Write about a long-term goal you're working towards. What steps can you take to stay motivated and persevere?

DAY 12

FAITH

SCRIPTURE: HEBREWS 11:1 DEFINES faith as trusting in God's unseen promises:

Now faith brings our hopes into reality and becomes the foundation needed to acquire the things we long for. It is all the evidence required to prove what is still unseen.

Reflection: How can you strengthen your faith in God?

Prayer: *Father, increase my faith. Help me to trust in Your promises, even when I can't see the outcome.*

Journaling Prompt: Write about a time when your faith was tested. How did you overcome your doubts and fears?

DAY 13

HOPE

SCRIPTURE: DAY 13: ISAIAH 40:31 reminds us of the renewal found in trusting God:

But those who wait for Yahweh's grace will experience divine strength. They will rise up on soaring wings and fly like eagles.

Reflection: How can you cultivate hope amid despair?

Prayer: *Father, fill me with hope. Help me to trust in Your goodness and mercy.*

Journaling Prompt: Write about a time when you lost hope. How did you find it again?

DAY 14

STRENGTH IN CHRIST

SCRIPTURE: PHILIPPIANS 4:13 DECLARES Christ's empowerment to overcome challenges.

And I find that the strength of Christ's explosive power infuses me to conquer every difficulty.

Reflection: Reflect on how relying on Christ's strength can empower you to overcome obstacles.

Prayer: *Father, thank You for being my strength in times of difficulty. Help me to rely on Your power to overcome challenges.*

Journaling Prompt: What is one obstacle you're currently facing? How can you rely on God's strength to push past it?

Week 2 Recap

This week centered on perseverance, resilience, and drawing strength from God during difficult seasons. You were reminded that setbacks do not define you and that endurance is built through faith and persistence.

This week focused on:

- Identifying obstacles that have challenged your progress
- Finding hope and strength in God during hardship
- Developing resilience and perseverance
- Remaining committed to long-term goals

Closing Reflection:
As you continue, remember that each step forward matters. With God as your strength, you are equipped to rise again and keep moving forward.

WEEK 3

Pivot

WEEK 3

CULTIVATING INNER PEACE

WELCOME TO WEEK THREE! This week centres on finding tranquillity and balance in a chaotic world. Key components include:

- Discovering peace amid life's storms
- Practicing gratitude
- Developing mindfulness and being present
- Learning to forgive
- Prioritizing self-care
- Exploring meditation and stillness
- Finding calm in God's presence

The daily exercises encourage you to slow down, reflect on your emotional and spiritual well-being, and develop practices that promote inner peace. The focus is on transforming perspective and finding joy through spiritual connection and self-awareness.

DAY 15

Finding Peace in the Storm

SCRIPTURE: PHILIPPIANS 4:7 ENCOURAGES resting in God's peace amid life's storms:

Then God's wonderful peace that transcends human understanding will make the answers known to you through Jesus Christ.

Reflection: How can you cultivate inner peace in a chaotic world?

Prayer: *Father, help me to find peace in Your presence, no matter what storms I may face.*

Journaling Prompt: Write about a time when you felt overwhelmed or anxious. How did you find peace in that moment?

DAY 16

Practicing Gratitude

Scripture: 1 Thessalonians 5:18 highlights gratitude as transformative:

And in the midst of everything be always giving thanks, for this is God's perfect plan for you in Christ Jesus.

Reflection: How can gratitude transform your perspective and bring you joy?

Prayer: *Father, help me to cultivate a heart of gratitude, and to focus on the blessings in my life.*

Journaling Prompt: List five things you are grateful for today.

DAY 17

MINDFULNESS

SCRIPTURE: PHILIPPIANS 4:7 COMPLEMENTS the theme of peace while offering a New Testament perspective:

"And the peace of God, which transcends all understanding, will guard your hearts and your minds in Christ Jesus." (NIV)

Reflection: How can you be more mindful of the present moment?

Prayer: *Father, help me to be present in the moment and to appreciate the simple joys of life.*

Journaling Prompt: Write about a time when you were fully present in the moment. How did it feel?

DAY 18

FORGIVENESS

SCRIPTURE: MATTHEW 6:14-15 STRESSES forgiveness as key to peace:

"And when you pray, make sure you forgive the faults of others so that your Father in heaven will also forgive you."

Reflection: How can you forgive those who have hurt you?

Prayer: *Father, help me to forgive others, as You have forgiven me.*

Journaling Prompt: Write about a time when you struggled to forgive someone. How did you eventually find forgiveness?

DAY 19

SELF-CARE

SCRIPTURE: MARK 6:31 ENCOURAGES prioritizing rest and renewal:

He said to them, "Come, let's take a break and find a secluded place where you can rest a while."

Reflection: How can you prioritize self-care in your busy life?

Prayer: *Father, help me to take care of my physical, emotional, and spiritual health.*

Journaling Prompt: Write about your self-care routine. What activities help you relax and recharge?

DAY 20

MEDITATION

SCRIPTURE: JOHN 14:27 EMPHASIZES Jesus' unique gift of peace, ideal for mindfulness and stillness:

"I leave the gift of peace with you—My peace. Not the kind of fragile peace given by the world, but My perfect peace. Don't yield to fear or be troubled in your hearts—instead, be courageous!"

Reflection: How can you use meditation to calm your mind and reduce stress?

Prayer: *Father, help me to find peace in Your presence through meditation and prayer.*

Journaling Prompt: Write about your meditation practice. What benefits have you experienced?

DAY 21

Be Still

SCRIPTURE: ISAIAH 26:3 PROVIDES encouragement to focus on trust in God to experience lasting peace:

"You will keep in perfect peace those whose minds are steadfast, because they trust in you." (NIV)

Reflection: Think about the power of being still in God's presence. How does this practice help you find peace?

Prayer: *Father, teach me to be still in Your presence. Help me to quiet my mind and find peace in knowing You are in control.*

Journaling Prompt: Take a moment of stillness today. Reflect on how it made you feel. Write about the experience.

Week 3 Recap

This week invited you to slow down and intentionally pursue peace in your mind and spirit. Through reflection and stillness, you explored practices that restore balance and renew your sense of calm.

This week encouraged you to:

- Seek peace in God's presence
- Practice gratitude and mindfulness
- Extend forgiveness and prioritize self-care
- Embrace stillness as a source of renewal

Closing Reflection:
Carry these practices with you as you move forward, allowing God's peace to anchor you through every season of life.

WEEK 4

Forward Momentum

WEEK 4

Embracing God's Purpose

Welcome to week four! The final week is about discovering and living out one's divine calling. Primary themes include:

- Uncovering God's purpose for one's life
- Stepping out in faith
- Surrendering control
- Finding purpose in challenges
- Serving others
- Living intentionally
- Embracing identity in Christ

This week challenges you to align your personal goals with God's plan, overcome fear, and live with purpose. The journaling prompts and reflections are designed to help you understand your unique calling and commit to living it out boldly and authentically.

DAY 22

Discovering Your God-Given Purpose

SCRIPTURE: JEREMIAH 29:11 ASSURES that God's plans are hopeful and purposeful:

"I know the plans I have for you," says the Lord. "They are plans for good and not for disaster, to give you a future and a hope."

Reflection: What is God's plan for your life? How can you discern His purpose for you?

Prayer: *Father, help me to discover Your purpose for my life, and to live it out with passion and dedication.*

Journaling Prompt: Take a moment of stillness today, then write about your dreams and aspirations. How can you align them with God's will?

DAY 23

STEPPING OUT IN FAITH

SCRIPTURE: JOSHUA 1:9 CALLS for courage and faith in God's presence:

This is My command—be strong and courageous! Do not be afraid or discouraged. For the Lord your God is with you wherever you go.

Reflection: How can you overcome fear and step out in faith?

Prayer: *Lord, give me the courage to step out of my comfort zone and into Your calling.*

Journaling Prompt: Write about a time when you had to step out in faith. What were the results?

DAY 24

SURRENDERING CONTROL

SCRIPTURE: PSALM 37:23-24 REASSURES that God supports those who follow Him:

The steps of a good man are ordered by the Lord, and He delights in his way. Though he fall, he shall not be utterly cast down; for the Lord upholds him with His hand.

Reflection: Consider a time when trusting God led you to clarity or peace. How can you deepen this trust?

Prayer: *Lord, I surrender my worries and uncertainties to You. Guide me as I trust You fully with my heart and actions.*

Journaling Prompt: Write about a moment when you struggled to trust God. What did you learn from that experience?

DAY 25

Purpose in Challenges

Scripture: Romans 8:28 affirms that God uses all things for good:

So we are convinced that every detail of our lives is continually woven together for good, for we are His lovers who have been called to fulfill His designed purpose.

Reflection: How has God used challenges in your life for good? Reflect on His faithfulness.

Prayer: Lord, thank You for working all things for my good. Help me to see Your hand in every season of my life.

Journaling Prompt: Reflect on a challenge you are facing now. How might God be using this to shape you for His purpose?

DAY 26

Serving Others

Scripture: Matthew 25:40 highlights serving others as serving Christ:

"When you cared for one of the least of these My little ones, My true brothers and sisters, you demonstrated love for Me."

Reflection: How can you serve others in a meaningful way?

Prayer: *Lord, help me to be a servant leader. Give me opportunities to bless others.*

Journaling Prompt: Write about a time when you served someone else. How did it make you feel?

DAY 27

Living Intentionally

Scripture: Ephesians 5:15-17 encourages intentional living aligned with God's will:

"So be very careful how you live, not being like those with no understanding, but live honorably with true wisdom."

Reflection: How can you live each day with intentionality?

Prayer: *Lord, help me to live each day with purpose. Give me the wisdom to prioritize my time and energy.*

Journaling Prompt: Write about your daily routine. How can you make it more intentional?

DAY 28

Embracing Your Identity in Christ

SCRIPTURE: 2 CORINTHIANS 5:17 celebrates the transformation of identity in Christ:

Now, if anyone is enfolded into Christ, he has become an entirely new person. All that is related to the old order has vanished.

Reflection: Who are you in Christ? How can you live out your identity as a child of God?

Prayer: *Lord, help me to embrace my identity in Christ. Give me the confidence to live boldly as Your child.*

Journaling Prompt: Write about the ways in which your identity in Christ has shaped your life.

Week 4 Recap

This final week focused on discovering your calling and living with intention and faith. You reflected on purpose, surrender, service, and your identity in Christ.

This week emphasized:

- Aligning your life with God's purpose
- Stepping out in faith and surrendering control
- Finding meaning in challenges
- Living intentionally and serving others

Closing Reflection:
As this journey concludes, remember that your purpose continues to unfold. Walk forward with confidence, trusting that God is guiding each step.

CLOSING MESSAGE

YOUR JOURNEY CONTINUES

REFLECTING ON 28 DAYS of Transformation

As you close the pages of this 28-day guided journal, take a moment to acknowledge the profound journey you've undertaken. These past weeks have been more than just a simple exercise in writing—they have been a transformative expedition of spiritual, personal, and professional growth. You've navigated through deep reflections, challenged your perspectives, and opened your heart to divine guidance.

The Ongoing Adventure of Growth

Remember that personal development is not a destination, but a continuous, dynamic journey. The principles of **PIvOT** and **PUSH** are not confined to these 28 days, but are powerful tools you can carry with you throughout your life. Each day presents new opportunities to:

PIvOT: Shift your perspective when challenges arise

PUSH: Persevere through obstacles with unwavering faith

Grow: Continuously learn and evolve

Nurturing the Seeds of Transformation

The wisdom you've gathered from scriptures, the moments of introspection, and the prayers you've uttered have planted seeds of transformation in your heart. These seeds—of faith, hope, resilience, and love—require consistent nurturing. Just as a gardener tends to their plants, you must:

- Water them with continued prayer and reflection
- Expose them to the sunlight of positive perspectives
- Protect them from the weeds of doubt and negativity
- Give them time to take root and flourish

Your Toolkit for Life's Challenges

The PIvOT and PUSH framework is more than a journal—it's a comprehensive approach to navigating life's complexities. You now possess a robust toolkit to:

- Reframe challenges as opportunities
- Maintain spiritual resilience
- Cultivate inner peace
- Align with your God-given purpose
- Move forward with confidence and grace

Continuing Your Exploration

Your journey doesn't end here. To deepen your understanding and continue your growth, consider:

Continued Journaling: Maintain the practice of daily reflection and spiritual writing

Deep Dive Resources:

- Read "PIvOT and PUSH: Embrace Change and Drive Forward on a Journey Beyond Limits"
- Explore additional resources at SRS Management and Leadership Consultancy
- **Community Support**: Share your insights, connect with like-minded individuals

Regular Self-Assessment: Periodically review your progress and realign with your spiritual goals

Final Encouragement

Trust that the work you've done over these 28 days has laid a strong foundation. The challenges you'll face are not obstacles, but opportunities for growth. Your faith, now deeper and more intentional, will be your compass.

Remember the core message: With God's guidance, you can **PIvOT** through any situation and **PUSH** beyond your perceived limitations.

Closing Prayer

Heavenly Father,

Thank You for this transformative journey. Continue to shape my heart, renew my mind, And guide my steps. May the seeds of faith planted during these 28 days Grow into a mighty forest of purpose and hope. In Your name, I pray.

Amen.

Your journey of growth, discovery, and spiritual transformation continues—one day, one moment at a time.

About the Author

Dr. Shamel Y. Rolle-Sands is a nurse leader, educator, researcher, and transformational leadership mentor with more than three decades of experience in healthcare and professional development.

She serves as the Director of the Public Hospitals Authority (PHA) Academy, leading initiatives in healthcare workforce education, clinical training, and leadership development across the public hospitals in The Bahamas. In this role, she champions the preparation of a competent, compassionate, and resilient health workforce committed to excellence in service and national development.

She will also serve as a facilitator in the upcoming inaugural Master of Science in Nursing (MSN) programme at the University of The Bahamas.

A passionate advocate for growth, resilience, and purpose-driven leadership, Dr. Rolle-Sands is also the founder of SRS Management and Leadership Consultancy, through which she empowers individuals and organizations to navigate change, pursue excellence, and lead with courage and conviction.

Grounded in faith and guided by service, her PIVOT and PUSH framework inspires others to persevere through life's challenges with discipline, determination, and unwavering belief in their God-given potential to transform adversity into purpose and impact.

Dr. Shamel Rolle-Sands
Chief Executive Officer
SRS Management and Leadership Consultancy

shamel.sands@gmail.com

UNIVERSAL IMPACT
PRESS

Made in the USA
Coppell, TX
11 May 2026

77016304R00056